C000299246

Maths

Assessment Papers
Up to Speed

8-9 years

OXFORD

UNIVERSITY PRESS

OXFORD
UNIVERSITY PRESS

Great Clarendon Street, Oxford, OX2 6DP, United Kingdom

Oxford University Press is a department of the University of Oxford.
It furthers the University's objective of excellence in research,
scholarship, and education by publishing worldwide. Oxford is a
registered trade mark of Oxford University Press in the UK and in
certain other countries

Text © Paul Broadbent 2015
Illustrations © Oxford University Press 2015

The moral rights of the authors have been asserted

First published in 2015

British Library Cataloguing in Publication Data
Data available

978-0-19-274094-6

10

Paper used in the production of this book is a natural, recyclable
product made from wood grown in sustainable forests.
The manufacturing process conforms to the environmental
regulations of the country of origin.

Printed in China

Acknowledgements

The publishers would like to thank the following for permissions to
use copyright material:

Page make-up: GreenGate Publishing Services, Tonbridge, Kent
Cover illustrations: Lo Cole

Although we have made every effort to trace and contact all
copyright holders before publication this has not been possible in all
cases. If notified, the publisher will rectify any errors or omissions at
the earliest opportunity.

Links to third party websites are provided by Oxford in good faith
and for information only. Oxford disclaims any responsibility for
the materials contained in any third party website referenced in
this work.

Introduction

What is Bond?

The Bond *Up to Speed* titles are part of the Bond range of assessment papers, the number one series for the 11+, selective exams and general practice. Bond *Up to Speed* is carefully designed to support children who need less challenging activities than those in the regular age-appropriate Bond papers, in order to build up and improve their techniques and confidence.

How does this book work?

The book contains two distinct sets of papers, along with full answers and a Progress Chart:

- Focus tests, accompanied by advice and directions, are focused on particular (and age-appropriate) maths question types encountered in the 11+ and other exams. The questions are deliberately set at a less challenging level than the standard *Assessment Papers*. Each Focus test is designed to help a child 'catch' their level in a particular question type, and then gently raise it through the course of the test and the subsequent Mixed papers.

- Mixed papers are longer tests containing a full range of maths question types. These are designed to provide rigorous practice with less challenging questions, perhaps against the clock, in order to help children acquire and develop the necessary skills and techniques for 11+ success.

Full answers are provided for both types of test in the middle of the book.

Some questions may require a ruler or protractor. Calculators are not permitted.

How much time should the tests take?

The tests are for practice and to reinforce learning, and you may wish to test exam techniques and working to a set time limit. Using the Mixed papers, we would recommend that your child spends 60 minutes answering the 50 questions in each paper.

You can reduce the suggested time by 5 minutes to practise working at speed.

Using the Progress Chart

The Progress Chart can be used to track Focus test and Mixed paper results over time to monitor how well your child is doing and identify any repeated problems in tackling the different question types.

Focus test 1 — Place value

Look at the value of each digit in a number:

2348

two thousand three hundred and forty-eight

2000 + 300 + 40 + 8

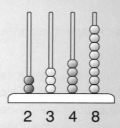

2 3 4 8

1 Write the missing numbers.

7483 = 7000 + 400 + _____ + _____

1685 = _____ + _____ + _____ + _____

2 Write these numbers as words.

6008 _____

_____

3970 _____

_____

Write the number shown on each abacus.

3

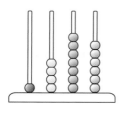

_____

4

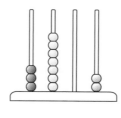

_____

3146 and 3416 use the same digits but they are very different numbers. Always check each digit when you write a number.

Circle the value of the 6 in each of these numbers.

5 9368   6000   600   60   6 $\frac{6}{10}$ $\frac{6}{100}$

6 37.6   6000   600   60   6 $\frac{6}{10}$ $\frac{6}{100}$

7 This is a 'divide by 10' machine.
Write the numbers coming out of the machine.

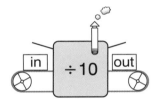

IN	2400	3000	7510	2660	4090
OUT	___	___	___	___	___

8 Write the number that is halfway on this number line.

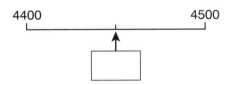

4400   4500

9 Round each number to the nearest 100.

458   rounds to _____

739   rounds to _____

10 Circle the number that is nearest to 600.

549   609   590   611   567

To round numbers to the nearest 100 look at the 'tens' digit:

- If it is 5 or more, round up the hundreds digit.

- If it is less than 5, the hundreds digit stays the same.

Doubles of numbers can be quite easy to work out —
so use them to work out near-doubles.

Example

14 + 14 = 28 so 14 + 15 is 1 more, which is 29.

1   Use doubles to answer these.

16 + 17 = _____   25 + 26 = _____   34 + 35 = _____

2   Write the missing numbers in this addition grid.

+	13	19
14	27	___
18	___	___

When you add numbers using a written method, make sure you line up
the columns carefully.

Example

What is 335 added to 492?

Step 1	Step 2	Step 3
2 + 5 = 7	90 + 30 = 120	400 + 300 + 100 = 800
4 9 2	4 9 2	4 9 2
+ 3 3 5	+ 3 3 5	+ 3 3 5
———	———	———
7	2 7	8 2 7
	1	1

Complete these calculations.

3 2 5 8
   + 3 9 5
   ————

4 3 6 7
   + 4 8 4
   ————

Jade bought a magazine for £3.20 and a chocolate bar for 65p.

5 How much did she spend in total? £_____

6 How much change did she get from £5? £_____

Try using a number line to count on to find the difference between numbers.

Example

What is the difference between 19 and 32?

Draw a blank number line from
19 to 32. Count on to 20, then
on to 32 to find the difference:

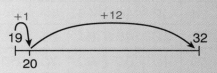

The difference between 19 and 32 is 13.

7 Find the difference between each pair of numbers.

47 ————————— 63 _____

56 ————————— 81 _____

8 Join each pair of numbers that has a difference of 8. There are three pairs to find.

   42   49   53   45   34   57

9 What is the difference between 39 and 72? _____

10 How much less is 48 than 84? _____

Try to learn all your tables facts. Use this grid to help you.

×	1	2	3	4	5	6	7	8	9	10	11	12
1	1	2	3	4	5	6	7	8	9	10	11	12
2	2	4	6	8	10	12	14	16	18	20	22	24
3	3	6	9	12	15	18	21	24	27	30	33	36
4	4	8	12	16	20	24	28	32	36	40	44	48
5	5	10	15	20	25	30	35	40	45	50	55	60
6	6	12	18	24	30	36	42	48	54	60	66	72
7	7	14	21	28	35	42	49	56	63	70	77	84
8	8	16	24	32	40	48	56	64	72	80	88	96
9	9	18	27	36	45	54	63	72	81	90	99	108
10	10	20	30	40	50	60	70	80	90	100	110	120

1 Complete these calculations.

$7 \times 2 = $ _____

$5 \times 5 = $ _____

$4 \times 6 = $ _____

$9 \times 4 = $ _____

$8 \times 5 = $ _____

Division is the opposite of multiplication. In maths we say 'division is the <u>inverse</u> of multiplication'.

$2 \times$ ____ $= 12$

____ $\times 2 = 12$

$12 \div$ ____ $= 6$

____ $\div 6 = 2$

2 This is a 'multiply by 3' machine. Write the missing numbers in the chart.

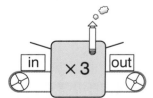

IN	2	____	4	____	9	____
OUT	6	24	____	21	____	30

3 Use each of these digits to complete the multiplications.

2   4   6   8

_____ × 5 = 20   _____ × _____ = 16   5 × _____ = 30

4 What is 13 multiplied by 3? _____

5 A ticket to see 'The Singing Superstars' in your local theatre costs £15.

How much will it cost in total for 4 tickets?

£_____

> Multiplying numbers up to 20 by a single digit can be worked out in your head.
>
> What is 14 multiplied by 5?
>
> • Multiply the tens: $10 \times 5 = 50$
> • Multiply the units: $4 \times 5 = 20$
> • Add the two parts: $50 + 20 = 70$

> To multiply tens by a single digit, work out the number fact and then make it ten times bigger:
>
> $60 \times 4 = 6 \times 4 \times 10 = 24 \times 10 = 240$

6 Work out the missing numbers. The first one has been done for you.

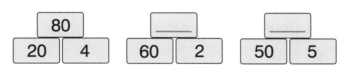

7 Write the missing numbers.

40 ÷ _____ = 10   _____ × 2 = 18

5 × _____ = 20   18 ÷ _____ = 3

8 There are 64 g of nuts in a bag. Half the nuts have been eaten.

How many grams of nuts are left? _____ g

9 36 footballs are grouped equally into 4 bags.

How many footballs are in each bag? _____

10 A box holds 3 light bulbs.

How many boxes are needed for 20 bulbs? _____

Focus test 4 Multiples and factors

A multiple is a number made by multiplying together two other numbers.

For example, 6 is a multiple of 2 because 3 x 2 = 6.

The multiples of 2 are 2, 4, 6, 8, 10... and so on.

1 Write the missing multiples of 4 up to 40.

4   8   _____   16   _____   24   _____   _____   _____   40

2 Look at these numbers.

21   24   16   18

Which numbers are multiples of 3? _____

Which number is a multiple of 7? _____

Which number is a multiple of both 4 and 6? _____

3 Circle the numbers from this set that are multiples of 5.

30 12 24 45 15 5 40 100

4 Use these digit cards to make four different multiples of 3.

_____ _____   _____ _____   _____ _____   _____ _____

5 Write each of these four numbers in the correct place on the Venn diagram.

25   18   12   16

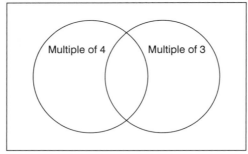

Factors are those numbers that will divide exactly in to other numbers. Factors of numbers can be put into pairs:

Factors of 21 → (1, 21) (3, 7) 21 has four factors.

Factors of 28 → (1, 28) (2, 14) (4, 7) 28 has six factors.

6 Write the missing factors of 30 in order.

30 → 1, 2, _____, _____, _____, _____, _____, _____

7 Now write the factors of 30 in pairs.

30 → (1, 30) (2, _____) (3, _____) (_____, _____)

8 Look at these numbers.

3   5   6   9

Which number is not a factor of 18? _____

Which number is not a factor of 45? _____

9 Write **always**, **sometimes** or **never** to make this sentence true.

A multiple of 6 is _____ an even number.

10 Write each of these four numbers in the correct place on this Venn diagram.

9   8   3   5

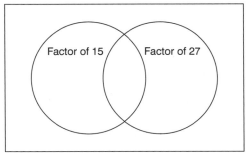

Now go to the Progress Chart to record your score!   Total ◯ 10

11

Fractions, decimals and percentages

Write the fraction of each shape that is shaded.

1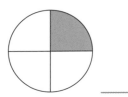

_____

2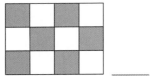

_____

3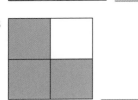

_____

A fraction has two parts:

$$\frac{3}{4}$$ ← numerator

← denominator

3 parts out of 4 are shaded.

This shows $\frac{3}{4}$.

The bottom number shows the number of equal parts in total. The top number shows how many equal parts to count.

Equivalent fractions are worth the same, even though they may look different.

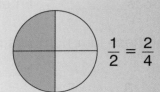

$$\frac{1}{2} = \frac{2}{4}$$

Circle **two** fractions in each set that have the same value as the first fraction.

Use the rectangles to help you.

4 $\frac{1}{2}$  $\frac{3}{6}$ $\frac{2}{5}$ $\frac{1}{10}$ $\frac{4}{8}$

5 $\frac{1}{4}$  $\frac{1}{6}$ $\frac{3}{12}$ $\frac{2}{8}$ $\frac{2}{10}$

6 Complete this equivalent fraction. $\frac{2}{10} = \frac{\square}{5}$

Percentages are simply fractions out of 100.

The percentage sign is %: per cent means 'out of 100'.

$\frac{1}{10}$	$\frac{1}{4}$	$\frac{1}{2}$	$\frac{3}{4}$
10%	25%	50%	75%

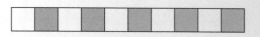

In this pattern, 5 squares are shaded.

$\frac{1}{2}$ or 50% of the squares are shaded.

The shaded section on this rectangle shows $\frac{1}{10}$.

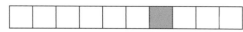

7 Circle the percentage that is shaded.

    10%   20%   25%   75%   50%

8 Shade more of the squares so that 50% is shaded in total.

Look at this circle to help you answer these questions.

9 What fraction of the circle is **not** shaded? _____

10 What percentage of the circle is shaded? Circle the answer.

    75%   25%   40%   80%   20%

Now go to the Progress Chart to record your score!   Total   10

Sequences

A sequence is a list of numbers in a pattern. Look at the difference between the numbers to work out the pattern.

Example

What is the next number in this sequence?

7   9   11   13   ____

Each number is 2 more than the previous number, so the next number is 15.

1 What are the missing numbers?

93   92   ____   90   89   ____   87   ____

What is the next number in each sequence?

2 3   6   9   12   ____

3 8   12   16   24   ____

4 Write the missing numbers on this grid.

1	2	3	___	5	___	___	8	9	10
11	___	13	___	___	16	___	___	___	20
21	22	___	___	___	___	27	___	29	___
31	___	___	___	35	___	___	38	___	___
___	42	___	___	___	46	___	48	___	50

5 Write the missing number in each sequence.

26   31   ____   41   46

160   210   ____   310   360

6 What are the next two numbers in this sequence?

525   530   535   540   545   ____   ____

7 In this sequence each number is double the previous number.

Write the missing numbers.

_____   6   12   24   _____   96

Write the missing numbers in each sequence.

8 147   150   _____   156   159   _____

9 99   88   _____   66   55   _____

10 What are the next three numbers in this sequence?

12   24   36   _____   _____   _____

Focus test 7 — Shapes and angles

Name these shapes.

1

_____

2

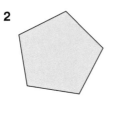

_____

3

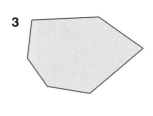

_____

A shape with straight sides is called a polygon. The name of the polygon tells you the number of sides:

3 sides	triangle	
4 sides	quadrilateral	
5 sides	pentagon	
6 sides	hexagon	
7 sides	heptagon	
8 sides	octagon	

Some shapes have lines of symmetry and are symmetrical. Look at this kite.

The dotted line is the line of symmetry. The shape on each side of the line is the same so the kite is symmetrical.

4 Draw the lines of symmetry on these shapes.

5 Draw a symmetrical triangle on this grid.

Show the line of symmetry with a dotted line.

Solid shapes are also called <u>3-dimensional</u> or <u>3-D</u> shapes.

Cube   Cuboid   Cylinder   Cone

Triangular prism   Sphere   Pyramid

6 Write the name of these shapes.

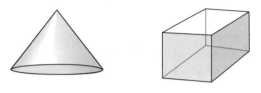

_____   _____

7 Cross out the shape that is **not** a pyramid.

8 What is the shape of each face of a cube? _____

Squares and rectangles have four right angles – one at each corner.

Put a dot in each right angle of these shapes.

9

10

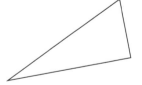

1 Draw a shape on this grid with an area of 12 squares.

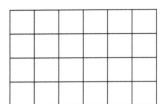

The area of a shape is the amount of surface that it covers. You can find the area of a shape by counting squares. If the shape is not made up from whole squares, count all the squares that are bigger than a half.

2 What is the area of this shape? _____ squares

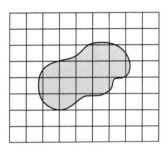

3 What is the area of this shape? _____ squares

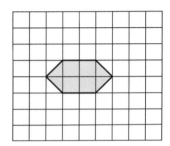

The area of a rectangle is length × width.

Example

4 cm

3 cm

Area = 3 cm × 4 cm = 12 square centimetres
Area is usually measured in square centimetres or square metres.

4 What is the area of this rectangle? _____ square centimetres

4 cm

9 cm

5 A rectangle has an area of 30 square centimetres. One side is 5 cm long.

What is the length of the other side? _____ cm

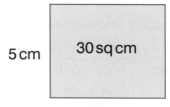

5 cm   30 sq cm

? cm

6 Draw a rectangle with an area of 24 square centimetres. Use a ruler.

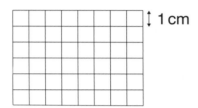   ↕ 1 cm

Calculate the perimeter of each rectangle.

The perimeter of a shape is the distance all the way around the edge. If the shape has straight sides, add up the lengths of all the sides.

2 cm

4 cm

Perimeter = 2 cm + 4 cm + 2 cm + 4 cm = 12 cm

3 cm

A   6 cm

5 cm

B   4 cm

7 Perimeter A = _____ cm

8 Perimeter B = _____ cm

9 Which shape has the larger area,

A or B? _____

10 What is the perimeter of the room shown in the diagram?

Perimeter = _____ m

9 m

6 m

Now go to the Progress Chart to record your score!   Total   10

19

Focus test 9   Measures

Length, weight (or mass) and capacity are all measured using different units.

Length	1 metre (m) = 100 centimetres (cm) 1 cm = 10 millimetres (mm) 1 kilometre (km) = 1000 m
Weight	1 kilogram (kg) = 1000 grams (g)
Capacity	1 litre (l) = 1000 millilitres (ml)

1 Change each of these lengths from metres into centimetres and into millimetres.

Metres	Centimetres	Millimetres
4 m	_____ cm	_____ mm
12 m	_____ cm	_____ mm

2 How many millilitres are there in 6 litres? _____ ml

3 How many grams are there in five and a half kilograms? _____ g

4 Write these amounts in order, starting with the smallest.

1500 ml   **2 litres**   **$1\frac{1}{4}$ litres**   **300 ml**

_____   _____   _____   _____

Smallest →

A scale is a row of marks to help us measure on a jug or ruler, for example. You need to read them carefully.

Look at the unit. Is it ml, cm, g...?

- If the level is in line with a mark, read off that number.
- If it is between numbers, work out what each mark means and count on or back.

20

5 Measure the sides of this rectangle with a ruler. Write down each measurement.

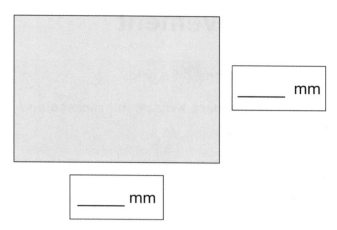

_____ mm

_____ mm

Read the scales and write how much water is in each jug.

6 _____ ml

7 _____ litres

8 Draw an arrow on the scale to show 650 grams.

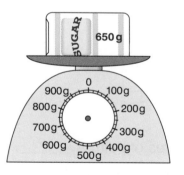

9 What is the most likely amount of water needed to fill a mug? Circle the answer.

30 litres   3 litres   30 ml   300 ml

10 What is the time shown on this clock? _____

Now go to the Progress Chart to record your score!   Total   10

21

Position and movement

Coordinates are used to show positions on a grid.

Coordinates are always pairs of numbers written in brackets and separated by a comma.

The number on the horizontal x-axis is written first, then the number on the vertical y-axis.

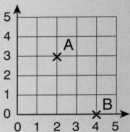

The coordinates of point A are (2, 3).

The coordinates of point B are (4, 0).

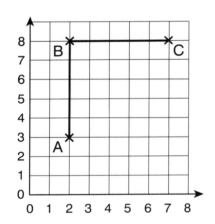

1 What are the coordinates of point A? (_____, _____)

2 What are the coordinates of point B? (_____, _____)

3 What are the coordinates of point C? (_____, _____)

4 A, B and C are three corners of a square. Mark the position of the fourth corner and label it D. Join the corners to make a square.

5 What are the coordinates of point D? (_____, _____)

Any answer that requires units of measurement should be marked wrong if the correct units have not been added.

Focus test 1

1 80 + 3, 1000 + 600 + 80 + 5
2 six thousand and eight, three thousand nine hundred and seventy
3 1476
4 3702
5 60
6 $\frac{6}{10}$
7 240, 300, 751, 266, 409
8 4450
9 500, 700
10 609

Focus test 2

1 33, 51, 69
2
+	13	19
14	27	**33**
18	**31**	37

3 653
4 851
5 £3.85
6 £1.15
7 16, 25
8 34 and 42; 45 and 53; 49 and 57
9 33
10 36

Focus test 3

1 14, 25, 24, 36, 40
2
IN	2	**8**	4	**7**	9	**10**
OUT	6	24	**12**	21	**27**	30

3 **4** × 5 = 20
   8 × 2 = 16 *or 2 ×* **8** = 16
   5 × **6** = 30
4 39
5 £60
6 120, 250
7 4, 9, 4, 6
8 32 g
9 9
10 7

Focus test 4

1 12, 20, 28, 32, 36
2 21, 24, 18; 21; 24
3 30, 45, 15, 5, 40, 100
4 *Any four of these*: 12, 15, 21, 24, 42, 45, 51, 54
5
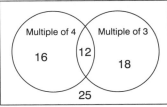

6 3, 5, 6, 10, 15, 30
7 (1, 30)   (2, **15**)
   (3, **10**)   (5, **6**)
8 5, 6
9 always
10
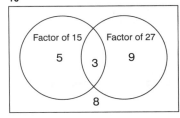

Focus test 5

1 $\frac{1}{4}$
2 $\frac{1}{2}$
3 $\frac{3}{4}$
4 $\frac{3}{6}, \frac{4}{8}$
5 $\frac{3}{12}, \frac{2}{8}$
6 $\frac{1}{5}$
7 10%
8 *Any 4* **more** *squares shaded*
9 $\frac{3}{4}$
10 25%

Focus test 6

1 91, 88, 86
2 15
3 28
4
1	2	3	**4**	5	**6**	**7**	8	9	10
11	**12**	13	**14**	**15**	16	**17**	**18**	**19**	20
21	22	**23**	**24**	**25**	**26**	27	**28**	29	**30**
31	**32**	**33**	**34**	35	**36**	37	38	**39**	**40**
41	42	**43**	**44**	**45**	46	**47**	48	**49**	50

5 36, 260
6 550, 555
7 3, 48
8 153, 162
9 77, 44
10 48, 60, 72

Focus test 7

1 rectangle *or* quadrilateral
2 pentagon
3 hexagon
4

5 *Check the triangle is symmetrical and has all the lines of symmetry marked – three lines for an equilateral triangle; one line for an isosceles triangle.*
6 cone, cuboid
7

8 square
9

10
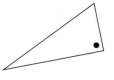

Focus test 8

1 Any shape covering 12 squares
2 14 squares
3 6 squares
4 36 square centimetres
5 6 cm
6 Any rectangle with an area of 24 sq cm that fits on the grid, e.g.: 3 cm × 8 cm, 4 cm × 6 cm or 6 cm × 4 cm
7 18 cm
8 18 cm
9 B
10 30 m

Focus test 9

1

Metres	Centimetres	Millimetres
4 m	**400** cm	**4000** mm
12 m	**1200** cm	**12 000** mm

2 6000 ml
3 5500 g
4 300 ml, $1\frac{1}{4}$ litres, 1500 ml, 2 litres
5 55 mm, 40 mm
6 350 ml
7 $2\frac{1}{2}$ litres
8

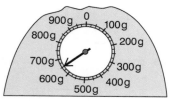

9 300 ml
10 10:20

Focus test 10

1 (2, 3)
2 (2, 8)
3 (7, 8)
4

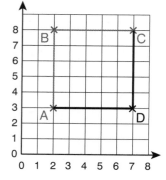

5 (7, 3)
6 east
7 north
8 north
9 south-east
10 north-east

Focus test 11

1 8
2 football
3 basketball
4 1
5 7
6 15
7 swing
8 38
9 12
10 jigsaws and bikes

Focus test 12

1–4

	Odd number	Not an odd number
Multiple of 5	35	40
Not a multiple of 5	37	28

5–8

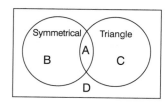

9–10 Check that the shapes drawn have the correct properties: i.e. a quadrilateral with one or more right angles; a shape that is not a quadrilateral and has no right angles, e.g. a scalene triangle or a regular pentagon.

Mixed paper 1

1–2 2350, 610
3 700
4 600
5 548
6 203
7 47
8 66
9 307
10–14

IN	7	**5**	3	4	9	**6**
OUT	28	20	**12**	16	**36**	24

15–16 3, 9
17–18 15, 27
19 B
20 A
21 =
22 >
23 35
24 50
25 200
26 68, 71, 73
27

28 cone
29 cuboid
30

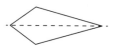

31 8 square centimetres
32 12 cm
33 25 square centimetres
34 20 cm
35 13 cm
36 1 m
37 8:15
38 8:45
39 (1, 5)
40 (4, 3)

41–42

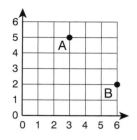

43 egg
44 7
45 2
46 25

47–50

	Odd number	Not an odd number
Multiple of 3	27	12
Not a multiple of 3	25	16

Mixed paper 2

1 895
2 909
3 400 *or* 4 hundred
4 $\frac{4}{10}$ *or* 4 tenths
5 £16.30
6 £3.70
7 51
8 13
9 96 ml
10–14 $3 \times 8 = 24$
$5 \times 6 = 30$ *or* $6 \times 5 = 30$
$4 \times 7 = 28$ *or* $7 \times 4 = 28$
15 4
16 25
17 21
18 32
19 25%
20 $\frac{2}{8}$
21 $\frac{3}{4}$
22 4
23–24 324, 524
25–26 1700, 1550
27 B
28 C
29 A
30 C
31 40 square metres
32 A and B have the same length perimeter.
33 B has a greater area than A.
34 10 m
35–38 2 g, 200 g, $\frac{1}{2}$ kg, 2 kg

39–40

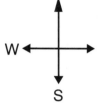

41–42

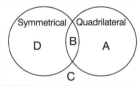

43 Mark
44 9
45 4
46 20

47–50

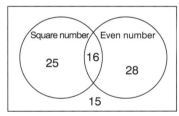

Symmetrical · Quadrilateral
D · B · A
C

Mixed paper 3

1 9910
2 9100
3 ÷
4 ×

5–7

+	45	63
27	72	**90**
46	**91**	**109**

8 221
9 21
10 27
11 7
12 80
13 8
14 28
15–17 1, 5, 25
18 sometimes
19 5
20 $\frac{2}{10}$ or $\frac{1}{5}$
21 50%
22 $\frac{2}{5}$

23 378
24 535
25–26 5, 80
27 sphere
28 cube
29 pentagon
30 2
31 *Check there is a line between A and C.*
32 *Check B and C are ticked.*
33 B
34 D
35 $1\frac{1}{4}$ litres
36 900 ml
37 550 cm
38 $\frac{3}{4}$ kg
39 (3, 2)
40

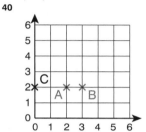

41 east
42 west
43 Mahmood
44 5
45 Jay
46 3
47–50

Square number · Even number
25 · 16 · 28
15

Mixed paper 4

1 £4
2 £8
3 ÷ 100
4 ÷ 10
5–7 74 and 65, 38 and 47, 70 and 61
8 15 cm
9 7.75 kg
10 £30
11 20
12 180
13 3
14 8

15 5
16 8
17 12
18 3 and 5
19 $\frac{3}{12}$
20–21 $\frac{2}{4}$, $\frac{6}{12}$
22 25%
23–24 109, 111
25 293
26 340
27 5 ml
28 C
29 B
30 A
31

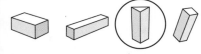

32 16 square centimetres
33 16 cm

34

‡1 cm

35 12 cm
36 $3\frac{1}{2}$ kg
37 600 g
38 7000 m
39

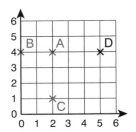

40 west
41 (2, 1)
42 D
43 3
44 Fish
45 4
46 17
47–50

	Even number of edges	Not an even number of edges
Triangular faces	B	C
No triangular faces	A	D

Learn the points of the compass.

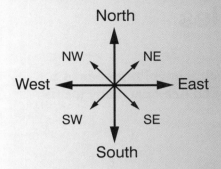

In between North, East, South and West are four other points. Their names always start with north or south.

Example: NE stands for north-east.

Clockwise means turning in the direction of the hands of a clock.

Anticlockwise means turning in the opposite direction.

- This arrow has moved a quarter turn clockwise.

- This arrow has moved a half turn anticlockwise.

Look at the compass points above to help you answer these questions.

6 If I face north and make a quarter turn clockwise, which direction will I be facing? _____

7 If I face south and make a half turn clockwise, which direction will I be facing? _____

8 If I face east and make a quarter turn anticlockwise, which direction will I be facing? _____

9 If I face north-west and make a half turn clockwise, which direction will I be facing? _____

10 If I face south-west and make a half turn anticlockwise, which direction will I be facing? _____

Charts, graphs and tables

Pictograms use symbols or pictures, where each symbol represents a certain number of items. Always check the key to see how many items each picture shows.

Example

Look at the pictogram below. Tennis was the least favourite sport. Only 2 children chose tennis.

These are the favourite sports for a group of children.

Favourite sport

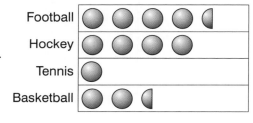

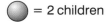 = 2 children

 = 1 child

1 How many children chose hockey? _____

2 Which sport was most children's favourite? _____

3 Which sport did 5 children choose? _____

4 How many more children chose football than chose hockey? _____

5 How many children chose tennis and basketball in total? _____

To understand bar charts and other types of graphs, look carefully at the different parts of the graph before you look at the bars.

- Read the title. What is it about?
- Look at the axis labels. These explain the lines that go across and up.
- Work out each scale. Does it go up in 1s, 2s, 5s, 10s...?

This chart shows the number of each type of toy sold in one week.

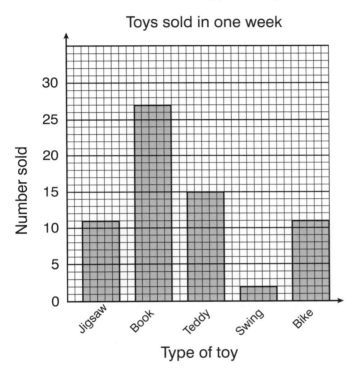

6 How many teddies were sold? _____

7 Which type of toy was sold twice? _____

8 How many books and jigsaws were sold in total? _____

9 How many more books were sold than teddies? _____

10 Two toys had the same number sold. Which toys were these?

_____ and _____

Venn diagrams and Carroll diagrams

A Venn diagram is like a sorting box with rings to sort out shapes, objects or numbers. Carroll diagrams do the same type of sorting as Venn diagrams, except they use a grid rather than circles.

These numbers have been sorted on a Venn diagram and a Carroll diagram. Compare the positions of the numbers.

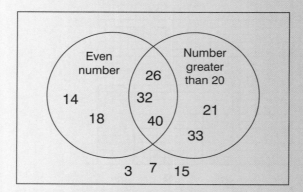

	Even number	Not an even number
Greater than 20	26 32 40	21 33
Not greater than 20	14 18	3 7 15

1–4 Write each number in the correct place on this Carroll diagram.

37   35   40   28

	Odd number	Not an odd number
Multiple of 5	_____	_____
Not a multiple of 5	_____	_____

5–8 Write the letter for each shape in the correct place on this Venn diagram.

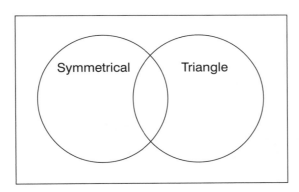

9–10 Draw two more shapes so there is a shape in each part of this Carroll diagram.

	1 or more right angles	No right angles
Quadrilateral		
Not a quadrilateral		

Now go to the Progress Chart to record your score!   Total   10

27

Mixed paper 1

1–2 Write the number that is halfway on each of these number lines.

2300   2400   560   660

2

Round each number to the nearest 100.

3 747 rounds to _____

4 582 rounds to _____

2

Complete these calculations.

5
```
   3 5 6
 + 1 9 2
 _____
```

6
```
   6 5 0
 − 4 4 7
 _____
```

2

This is how children travel to school.

Walking	Car	Bus
49 children	162 children	96 children

7 How many more children travel by bus than walk to school? _____

8 How many more children travel to school by car than bus? _____

9 How many children are there in the school in total? _____

3

10–14 This is a 'multiply by 4' machine.

Write the missing numbers in the chart.

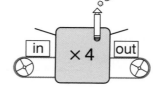
in   × 4   out

IN	7	___	3	___	9	___
OUT	28	20	___	16	___	24

5

15–16 Write the missing factors of 18.

18 → 1, 2, _____, 6, _____, 18

2

17–18 Write the missing multiples of 3.

3   6   9   12   _____   18   21   24   _____   30

2

Look at the shaded section in these circles.

A   B   C

19 Which shape has $\frac{1}{2}$ shaded? _____

20 Which shape has $\frac{1}{3}$ shaded? _____

2

Write <, > or = to make each statement true. Look at the circles to help you.

21 $\frac{1}{3}$ _____ $\frac{2}{6}$

22 $\frac{1}{2}$ _____ $\frac{1}{6}$

> Remember:
>
> < means 'is less than'
>
> > means 'is greater than'
>
> = means 'equal to'

2

Write the next number in each sequence.

23 23   26   29   32   _____

24 66   62   58   54   _____

25 40   80   120   160   _____

3

26 What are the missing numbers?

67   _____   69   70   _____   72   _____

1

27 Cross out the shape that is **not** a rectangle.

1

29

Join each shape to the correct name.

| Prism | Cube | Cone | Sphere | Pyramid | Cuboid |

28

29

30 Draw a line of symmetry on this shape.

Calculate the area and perimeter for each of these.

31 Area = _____ square centimetres

32 Perimeter = _____ cm

2 cm

4 cm

33 Area = _____ square centimetres

34 Perimeter = _____ cm

5 cm

5 cm

35 What is the length of this line in centimetres? _____ cm

36 What is the most likely height of a table? Circle the answer.

1 km   1 cm   1 m   1 mm

Write your answers using numbers.

37 What is the time shown on this clock? _____

38 What is the time half an hour later? _____

2

1

4

1

1

2

39 What are the coordinates of point A?
Circle the answer.

(5, 0)   (1, 5)   (1, 0)   (5, 1)

40 Write the coordinates of point B. (_____, _____)

41–42 Label the arrows pointing north and
east with the letters N and E.

A group of children were asked in a survey to choose their favourite type of
sandwich: egg, jam or cheese. The results are shown in this pictogram.

Favourite sandwich filling

43 Which type of sandwich is most children's favourite? _____

44 How many children's favourite filling is cheese? _____

45 How many more children chose egg than jam as their favourite? _____

46 How many children in total took part in this survey? _____

47–50 Write each number in the correct section of the Carroll diagram.

27   **16**   **12**   **25**

	Odd number	Not an odd number
Multiple of 3	_____	_____
Not a multiple of 3	_____	_____

Mixed paper 2

Circle the number in each group that is nearest to 900.

1 879   911   910   890   895

2 927   887   920   975   909   2

Write the value of the 4 in each of these numbers.

3 6435   _____

4 12.4   _____   2

David bought sunglasses for £5.80 and a hat for £10.50.

5 How much did he spend in total? £_____

6 How much change did he get from £20? £_____   2

Complete these calculations.

7 25 + 26 = _____

8 32 − 19 = _____   2

9 What is the difference between 234 ml and 330 ml? ____ ml   1

10–14 Use each of these digits once to complete the multiplications.

4   5   6   7   8

3 × _____ = 24   _____ × _____ = 30   _____ × _____ = 28   5

15 Write the missing factor of this square number.

16   →   1, 2, _____, 8, 16   1

Look at these numbers.

14   25   32   21

16 Which number is a multiple of 5? _____

17 Which number is a multiple of 3? _____

18 Which number is a multiple of 4? _____   3

The shaded section on this rectangle shows $\frac{1}{4}$.

19 Circle the percentage that is shaded.

10%   20%   25%   40%   50%

20 Circle the fraction that is the same as $\frac{1}{4}$

$\frac{4}{8}$ $\frac{2}{8}$ $\frac{1}{8}$ $\frac{1}{2}$

21 Circle the fraction of the shape that is **not** shaded.

$\frac{1}{4}$ $\frac{4}{8}$ $\frac{3}{4}$ $\frac{2}{8}$ $\frac{2}{4}$

22 How many squares in total on this shape would be shaded to show $\frac{1}{2}$?

_____

4

Write the missing numbers in each sequence.

23–24 124   224   ____   424   ____   624

25–26 1750   ____   1650   1600   ____   1500

4

Look at these triangles. Write the letter of the correct shape for each answer.

27 Which triangle is symmetrical? _____

28 Which triangle has a right angle? _____

29 Which triangle has an obtuse angle? _____

3

30 Which of these shapes is a cylinder? _____

1

31 A room is 8 m long and 5 m wide.

What is the area of the room? _____ square metres

1

Look at these two rectangles. Underline one statement in each question that is true.

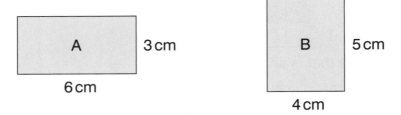

A 3 cm 6 cm

B 5 cm 4 cm

32 A has a longer perimeter than B.

B has a longer perimeter than A.

A and B have the same length perimeter.

33 A has a greater area than B.

B has a greater area than A.

A and B have the same size area.

○ 2

34 A pond is 3 m long and 2 m wide. It has a path all the way round.

How long is the path? ____ m

○ 1

35–38 Write these weights in order, starting with the lightest.

200 g $\frac{1}{2}$ kg   2 kg   2 g

_____   _____   _____   _____

Lightest →

○ 4

Plot each point in the correct position on the grid and label it with its letter.

39 A (3, 5)

40 B (6, 2)

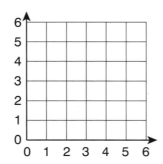

○ 2

41–42 Label the arrows pointing south and west with the letters S and W.

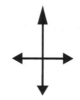

◯ 2

This graph shows the scores in a spelling test.

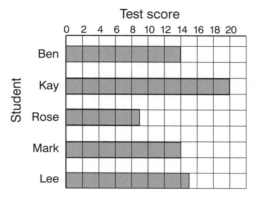

43 Who got the same score in the test as Ben? _____

44 What was Rose's score? _____

45 How many students scored over 10 marks in the test? _____

46 One student spelt all the words in the test correctly.

How many words were there in the spelling test? _____

◯ 4

47–50 Write the letter for each shape in the correct part of the Venn diagram.

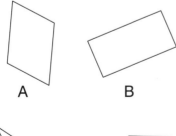

A   B

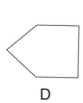

C   D

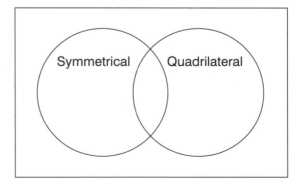

◯ 4

Mixed paper 3

Write the number that is one more than each of these.

1 9909 _____

2 9099 _____

2

Write × or ÷ to make each statement true.

3 146 ____ 10 = 14.6

4 25.8 ____ 100 = 2580

2

5–7 Write the missing numbers in this addition grid.

+	45	63
27	72	____
46	____	____

3

Answer these.

8 What is 89 added to 132? _____

9 What is 500 take away 479? _____

2

Work out these.

10 Multiply 3 by 9. _____

11 Divide 35 by 5. _____

12 What is 4 multiplied by 20? _____

3

13 Three children share a bag of 24 sweets equally between them.

How many sweets will each child have? _____

14 A rabbit eats 4 carrots a day.

How many carrots will the rabbit eat in one week? _____

2

15–17 Write the factors of 25.

25 → _____, _____, _____

3

18 Write **always**, **sometimes** or **never** to make this sentence true.

A multiple of 5 is _____ an odd number.

1

Look at this rectangle to help you answer these questions.

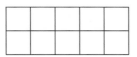

19 What is $\frac{1}{2}$ of 10? _____

20 Write 20% as a fraction. _____

21 What is $\frac{1}{2}$ as a percentage? _____%

22 Complete this equivalent fraction.

$$\frac{4}{10} = \frac{\Box}{5}$$

4

Write the missing number in each sequence.

23 372   374   376   _____   380

24 545   540   _____   530   525

2

25–26 In this sequence each number is double the previous number.

Write the missing numbers.

_____   10   20   40   _____   160

2

Write the name of each shape.

27

_____

28

_____

2

Look at this shape.

29 What is this shape called? _____

30 How many right angles are there in this shape? _____

2

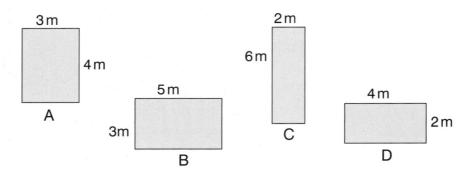

31 Draw a line to join the two shapes with the same size area.

32 Tick the two rectangles with the same length perimeter.

33 Which shape has the largest area? _____

34 Which shape has the shortest perimeter? _____

Write the amount of water in each jug.

35

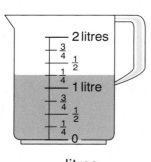

_____ litres

36

_____ ml

37 What is $5\frac{1}{2}$ m in centimetres? _____ cm

38 Which is heavier, $\frac{3}{4}$ kg or 700 g? _____

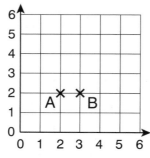

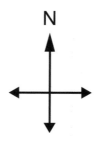

39 What are the coordinates of point B? Circle the answer.

(3, 3)   (2, 0)   (2, 3)   (3, 2)

40 Point C is at (0, 2). Plot this point and label it.

41 You are standing at A and looking towards B. Which direction are you facing? Circle the answer.

north　　　　　　　**east**　　　　　　　**south**　　　　　　　**west**

42 You are standing at A and looking towards C. Which direction are you facing? Circle the answer.

north　　　　　　　**east**　　　　　　　**south**　　　　　　　**west**

〇 4

This pictogram shows the number of books read in one month.

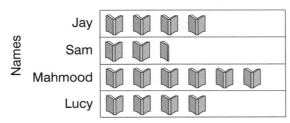

Book reading

43 Who read the most books? _____

44 How many books did Sam read? _____

45 Who read the same number of books as Lucy? _____

46 How many more books did Jay read than Sam? _____

〇 4

47–50 Write these numbers in the correct section of the Venn diagram.

15　　　　**16**　　　　**28**　　　　**25**

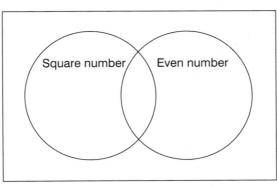

〇 4

Mixed paper 4

Round each amount to the nearest £1.

1 £4.39   £_____

2 £7.60   £_____

Write ÷ **10** or ÷ **100** to make each statement true.

3 1430 _____ = 14.3

4 7 _____ = 0.7

5–7 Join pairs of numbers with a difference of 9.

74   38   70   65

61   47

8 Kate is 163 cm tall and her sister is 148 cm tall.

How much taller is Kate than her sister? _____ cm

9 A shopping basket has a 1.5 kg bag of washing powder, 5 kg of potatoes and a 1.25 kg bag of rice.

What is the total weight of shopping in the basket? _____ kg

10 A train ticket costs £5.

How much will it cost for 6 people to travel by train? £_____

Write the missing numbers.

11 8 × _____ = 160

12 _____ ÷ 30 = 6

13 40 × _____ = 120

14 A class of 32 children is divided equally into 4 teams.

How many children are there in each team? _____

Look at these numbers.

2   3   4   5   6   8   12

15 Which number is not a factor of 24? _____

16 Which number is not a factor of 60? _____

17 Which number is a multiple of 2, 3 and 4? _____

18 Which numbers are not multiples of 2? _____

Look at this circle to help you answer these questions.

19 Circle the fraction that is the same as $\frac{1}{4}$.

$\frac{4}{10}$ $\frac{3}{12}$ $\frac{4}{12}$ $\frac{3}{4}$ $\frac{2}{12}$

20–21 Circle **two** fractions that are the same as $\frac{1}{2}$.

$\frac{2}{4}$ $\frac{4}{12}$ $\frac{1}{3}$ $\frac{6}{12}$ $\frac{1}{6}$

22 Circle the percentage of the circle that is not shaded.

30%   25%   40%   10%   50%

23–24 Write the missing numbers in this sequence.

108   _____   110   _____   112   113

Write the missing number in these sequences.

25 289   291   _____   295   297

26 400   380   360   _____   320

27 What is the most likely amount of water that a teaspoon can hold? Circle the answer.

500 ml   5 litres   50 ml   5 ml

4

4

2

2

1

41

Look at these shapes. Write the letter of the correct shape for each answer.

28 Which shape is not symmetrical? _____

29 Which shape is not a triangle? _____

30 Which shape is an equilateral triangle? _____

31 Circle the shape that is the odd one out.

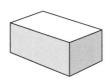 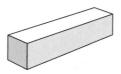  

What is the area and perimeter of this square?

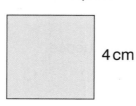

4 cm

32 Area = _____ square centimetres

33 Perimeter = _____ cm

34 Draw a square with an area of 9 square centimetres. Use a ruler.

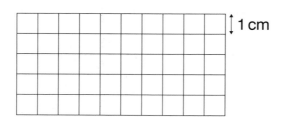

1 cm

35 What is the perimeter of the square you have drawn? _____ cm

Write the weight of each parcel.

36 _____ kg

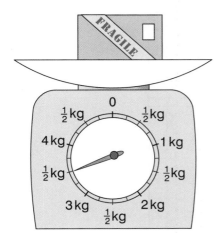

37 _____ g

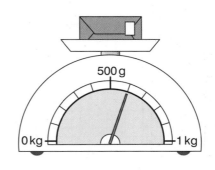

38 What is 7 km in metres? _____ m

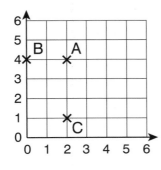
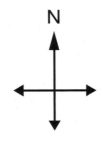

39 Point D is at (5, 4). Plot this point and label it.

40 You are standing at A and looking towards B. Which direction are you facing? Circle the answer.

north   **south**   **west**   **east**

41 What are the coordinates of point C? (_____, _____)

42 Which point is east of point A? _____

This bar chart shows the number of pets in a shop.

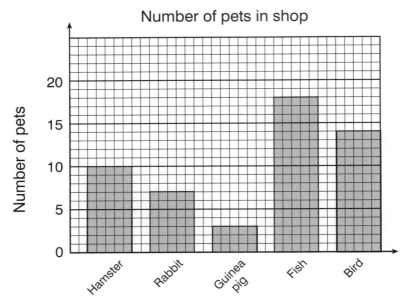

Number of pets in shop

43 How many guinea pigs does the pet shop have? _____

44 Which type of pet does the shop have most of? _____

45 How many more fish than birds are there in the shop? _____

46 How many hamsters and rabbits are there in total? _____

4

47–50 Write the letter for each shape in the correct part of the Carroll diagram.

A

B

C

D

	Even number of edges	Not an even number of edges
Triangular faces	_____	_____
No triangular faces	_____	_____

4